STOP
painting red flags white

Hustle 101
Motivational Speakers & Mentoring Program
Proven Life Changers

Santiego Rivers

STOP
painting red flags white

Copyright © 2021 by **Santiego Rivers**

All rights reserved. This book may not be reproduced or transmitted in any form without the written permission of the author.

"no copyright infringement is intended."

ISBN 978-1-7370516-9-5

A person will tell you everything you need to know about them within the first few minutes of meeting them. Will you take the time to listen?

It is not always the verbal cues that reveal a person's motive. Instead, it is often their actions that speak louder than their words.

Their words don't always match their actions, especially when they intend to deceive you. It is not their fault when we do not take the needed percussions to protect our hearts from our deceitful eyes.

Our deceitful eyes entice us to give in to our wants as we sacrifice what we need.

We focus more on our **wants** than our **needs** which always leave us praying on our knees.

We stop asking questions about what we **need** to know about a person because we are too afraid to mess up what we think we **want** from that person.

No one can fill a void in your life but you!

All journeys for self-discovery must start from within us. When you begin trying to discover what is missing from your life by finding it in other people, you will surely fail.

No one can fill a void in your life but you!

You don't need anyone to help make your life happy or complete.

If you search for happiness from another person, you will endure a lifetime of misery and despair.

A beautiful face, a nice body, or all the money in the world will never substitute being equally yoked with a person in a healthy relationship.

Just ask the wives of *Bill Gates* or *Jeff Bezos* or the many husbands of *Halle Berry* or *Mariah Carey*.

This book will examine the many red flags that people will reveal to us, but we choose to ignore them and paint them white.

You will notice many situations within this book that you have encountered dealing with other people and a few situations that will prepare you for future encounters.

This book will give you the tools to make sure that you are not sacrificing your **needs** because of your **wants**.

*A narcissist will get to know you so that they can find ways to control you through your weakness.

*A vampire/ energy drainer searches for positive people so that they can drain your energy.

Be cautious of these two types of people!

Table of Content

- What are "Red Flags?"
- Lack of communication
- Irresponsible, immature, and unpredictable
- Lack of trust
- Significant family and friends don't like your partner
- Controlling behavior
- Feeling insecure in the relationship
- A dark or secretive past
- Non-resolution of past relationships
- Closing Statement

What are "Red Flags"?

"Red Flags" are the things that other people say or do that should cause us to walk away from them immediately.

Our misleading eyes ignore all the warning signs that our mind and spirit feel and makes us proceed without caution.

We paint all of those **"Red Flags"** white with reckless abandon because we want our eyes to be right despite our mind and spirit knowing it's very wrong.

Loneliness makes us ignore many of the traits that others may possess that are not right for us and our well-being.

We settle for being wanted and desired now that we risk our future mental and physical well-being.

We tell ourselves that maybe we misheard what they said or the signs that we noticed were incorrect.

But, months or years into a toxic relationship, we are stuck trying to make it work because we don't want to admit to ourselves or other people that we choose the wrong person to be in our lives.

So, what are some of the **"Red Flags"** that should never be painted white?

Here are some critical relational red flags to look out for:

- Lack of communication
- Irresponsible, immature, and unpredictable
- Lack of trust
- Significant family and friends don't like your partner
- Controlling behavior
- Feeling insecure in the relationship
- A dark or secretive past
- Non-resolution of past relationships

Lack of communication – The main problem with this "Red Flag" is not the lack of communication part. The problem occurs when the other person is unwilling to work on it to work for both of you.

Yes, I said for the both of you!!!

Women are primarily emotional beings, and Men are primarily logical beings. I used the word **"primarily"** because there are always exceptions to the rule.

I am sure that we all know of some logical-thinking women and some emotional-feeling men.

We need to find a way to ensure that both parties get what they need from the relationship, as it involves being heard and understood.

Good communication will take a lot of work to develop and maintain within any "Working" relationship.

Many businesses and big corporations focus on building and maintaining communication at their facility.

Hopefully, if you did premarital marriage counseling, your counselor informed you that your marriage will always be a "working" marriage.

Your marriage will be more challenging than your job because it is a seven-day-a-week, twenty-four hours a day commitment.

The main thing you need to understand when communicating with someone you love is that you love them.

When you truly love someone, there is a respect factor that shows in what you do and what you say to that other person.

Without respect in a relationship, there is no love...

If you try to get someone to understand why you are right in an argument, you have already failed.

Many of us fail to understand this one key point when it comes to building good communication with someone.

What is the point of being right in an argument if you both are not getting what you need from the other person?

Are you trying to win an argument, or are you trying to improve your communication skills with that other person?

You cannot do both. Instead, you must decide which one of the two things you are more concerned with because they will take you down two different paths.

If you are trying to win an argument, you will only succeed in pushing the other person away because you are not giving them what they want/ need from you, which is understanding how they feel and how you may have made them feel.

If you care more about improving your communication with that person, your first action should be to listen for clarity about how they feel inside and what you may have done to cause this feeling.

Next, you should assure them that you understand what they are telling you, and you want to know what you can do to make the situation better.

I don't recommend trying to justify things from your perspective. You will only succeed in making the situation worse.

If you can give a person what they want, you will have a higher chance of that other person giving you what you need.

Someone willing to communicate with you because they feel that you listen to their concerns.

I.I.U

Irresponsible, immature, and unpredictable

Avoid being in a relationship with anyone who suffers from being **I.I.U.**

Treat these individuals like someone who has an incurable disease that wants to share it with the world.

You will never get what you consistently need from an irresponsible, immature, and unpredictable person.

Of course, occasionally, they may rise to the occasion, but remember I

said the keyword earlier, which is **"consistent**."

Most of the people who suffer from being **I.I.U** are very beautiful. But, unfortunately, their looks are why we often overlook all their bad qualities.

We tell ourselves that we are just going to enjoy the moment with these types of people, but months or even years later, we are still involved in a toxic relationship with those individuals.

How can we honestly blame someone else for the things that we allow them to do to us?

I don't know how we can honestly do it, but we always find a way to shift the blame.

We tell ourselves that the person did not initially show signs of being irresponsible, immature, and unpredictable.

But, were those signs "Red Flags" that we painted white because we were caught up in the moment?

The one question that we probably do not ask someone that is very important when we meet them is why they are single?

The answer to that question is very crucial when it comes to getting to know if that other person is right for you.

When a guy or girl claims that all their past lovers took advantage of them, end the date immediately. In their words, they are too nice, too trusting, too giving, or simply too much of a good thing.

What people say and the reality of the situation does not always line up the same way. A relationship is a union. One person will never be the reason that a relationship lasts or fail.

Anyone who spends their time blaming the other person for a failed relationship is likely the main reason the relationship did not work.

Rather it was directly or indirectly; the accuser played a significant role in the relationship's demise.

After any failed event in our lives, we should always learn to do an honest assessment in the end.

An honest assessment will allow us to re-examine some of the mistakes that we made and learn what we need to fix moving forward to ensure that it was a mistake that we made and not flaws in our character that we need to address.

If you can't find the flaws in you that caused you to be single, you may want to seek counseling immediately before engaging in another relationship with anyone!

Lack of trust

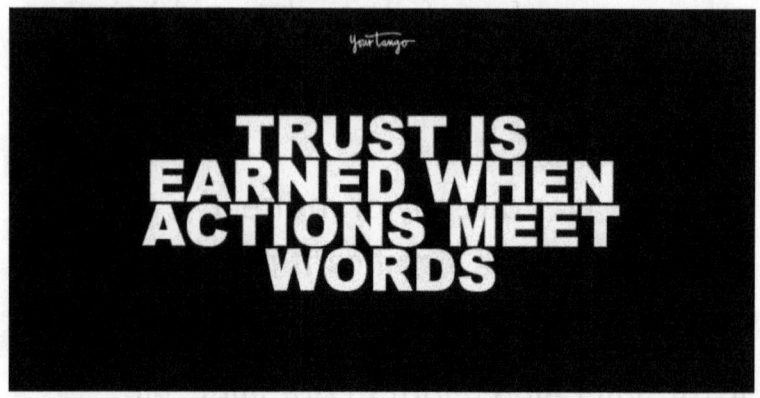

You must understand the following when it comes to trust.

- Trust means trusting yourself
- Trusting your judgments
- Trusting others

Trust is the foundation for any relationship. Without it, the relationship will be shaky and will eventually come to an end.

Trust means you can rely on your partner when time gets tough, and you can confide in them and feel safe with them.

Trust your mind and your soul before you trust your deceiving eyes. Doing this will help you build trust in yourself and the decisions that you make.

People are self-serving creatures. The trick to picking the right person to be in your life is to make sure that your interests and desires are the same. Create a checklist based upon the things that your mind and heart need fulfilled and not just your eyes.

We should all have a checklist of the things that we want a person to fulfill off our list.

A checklist is very similar to when you are applying for a job. Your future employee will tell you the qualifications they are looking for and ask you to provide them with references.

Why not do the same when it comes to your personal life? Take the time to develop a checklist that you want the other person to come close to completing. Of course, no one will fulfill everything on your list.

Sometimes before you get the job that you are pursuing, you may have to do several interviews.

When it comes to checking their references; You may not be able to talk to their exes, but you can ask them about their past relationships and get a feel of what type of person you are dealing with.

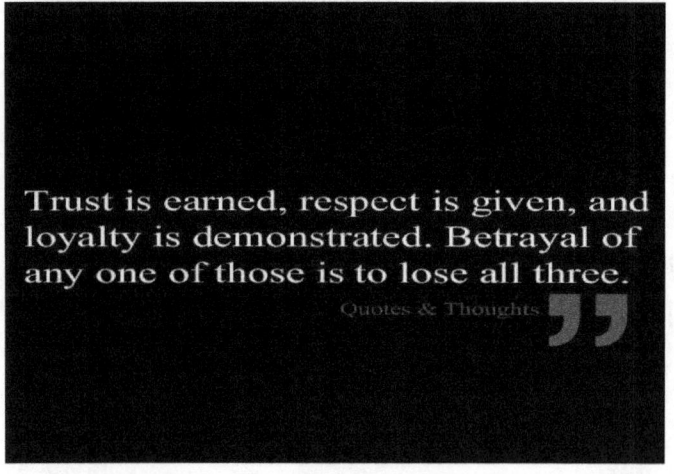

You should expect honesty above all else. So, put people in a situation that requires them to be honest with you.

Are you sexually attracted to me?

This one question will let you know everything that you need to know about being able to consider trusting that other person.

Don't be afraid of talking about sex because we are physical beings. When we meet someone, there must first be a physical attraction that makes us want to know more about them.

Talking about sex helps remove the elephant in the room and open the door for a deeper conversation.

Trust takes a level of vulnerability that both parties must be willing to share. You should trust a person with your heart before you bless them with sharing your body.

It's all about trust

Yes, having sex with someone should be considered a blessing because you are sharing something special with them.

Intimacy is not sex. Learn the difference between both words. Sex and intimacy should require a high level of trust that takes time to build.

> **TRUST TAKES YEARS TO BUILD, SECONDS TO BREAK, AND FOREVER TO REPAIR.**

Significant family and friends don't like your partner

The keyword is **"significant"** family and friends. You must make sure that you understand what the word **"significant"** means and how to apply it to your life.

Sig ·nif·i·cant - sufficiently great or important to be worthy of attention

In theory, we expect our family members to have our best interests in mind, including our friends, but this is not always the case for some people.

You should know the true dynamic of your relationship with your family and your friends if you are not in denial.

As I mentioned earlier, people are self-serving creatures.

Do your interests align with each other?

If you have family or friends who are jealous of you and are trying to live their life through you, how can you expect them to accept someone new in your life that encourages you to grow as a person?

It doesn't help if you have other issues you are dealing with because of your family dynamics.

I pray that you seek help before the *vampires* in your life take away something that made your life better for you.

If you are fortunate to have **"significant"** people in your life, seek their guidance and wisdom because they know your strengths and weaknesses, which will help you on your path.

Don't worry!

It's normal if you don't like your partner's family, and it's completely normal not to have a close moment every time you see and spend time together.

I am sure that they do not like all their family members also. Family dynamics are a lot, especially when dealing with a family that is not your own.

I recommend being cordial and respectful and know when to remove yourself from an uncomfortable situation.

You can do the same thing when it comes to your partners' friends. You should know the type of people who will make you act out of character

Controlling behavior

5 Warning Signs of an Unhealthy Relationship

- You are feeling isolated. Feeling distanced from the people you care about because of your relationship is a **red flag**.
- Excessive jealousy.
- Deflecting responsibility and blame. Frequent arguments.
- Trying to change each other

Any one of these things is **"Red Flags"** that should never be painted white.

Your partner should never make you feel that you are not allowed to spend time away from them. All healthy relationships need space.

Excessive jealousy is never a good thing. Although a bit of jealousy is expected when our feeling is involved, we are human.

> **"Mild jealousy can be healthy**," says Dr. Magavi.

He feels that It reiterates that individuals care about their partners, value them, and do not want to lose them.

Take the time to understand the difference and ensure that you are doing the things to ensure that your mate knows that they are happy being in a relationship with you.
(Communication)

Deflecting responsibility and blame/ frequent arguments

Disagreements are healthy. But when your partner blames every argument on something you said or did, they're deflecting responsibility.

It takes two people to argue

That statement has not changed since the publication of this book.

It should never be about what someone else did. The only thing that should matter is how we responded to the situation. No matter what's going on in someone's life, they're still responsible for their actions, especially when their actions affect their partner.

When you are arguing with your spouse, remember how you feel about them. Being upset will never justify how you made them feel inside.

We must learn how to fight fairly and respectfully. Learn how to start your conversation with something positive before you move into what is bothering you.

"Honey, I love you first and foremost."

No one wants to hear negative things constantly. Make sure you discuss one thing at a time and get closer before you move onto the following topics. Don't keep bringing up old stuff unless that person is not working to fix it.

Be mindful of the following tactic

When you try talking to your partner about something they did that bothered you, they'll say things like, "You're too sensitive," or, "It was just a joke."

This tactic turns your attention away from their behavior and makes you question your feelings instead.

In a healthy relationship, you accept responsibility when you do something to upset your partner. You apologize and work on changing your behavior to make sure it doesn't happen again. Would you please make sure that you notice the effort of your partner?

It's hard to accept the negative parts of ourselves and our capacities to hurt one another, especially when we have been doing this for a long time.

It's essential to take ownership of our actions. Learning to own one's mistakes and shortcomings is crucial for a healthy, fulfilling relationship.

Trying to change each other

Encouraging someone to be their best self is an admirable quality of a supportive partner, but forcibly trying to change your spouse can do more damage than good.

It would help if you learned the difference between being an encouraging partner and a forceful one. Unfortunately, we often paint this **"Red Flag"** white because we confuse the two things initially.

You may go into a relationship hoping that your spouse will mature and change their mind over time about many things you disagree with but trying to change their views is something else.

Why do they have to change, allowing you to stay the same?

Where is the compromise? Putting yourself on a mission to change your spouse is highly disrespectful to them and your relationship.

It takes time for a flower to bloom and a seed to grow. So, in the meantime, focus on loving that person and giving them what they want so that they will be able to provide you with what you need from them in time.

If you constantly try to change your partner, you essentially tell them that what they must offer you isn't good enough. That type of behavior can push them away and cause distance in the relationship.

How much do you value what you have with the other person?

Feeling insecure in the relationship

You must understand that insecurity is an inner feeling of being threatened and inadequate in some way.

Most relationship insecurities are from the irrational thoughts and fears that we hold onto that are not present.

We fear that we are not good enough, that we will not be okay without a partner in our life, that we will never find anyone better, or that we are not genuinely lovable.

You are all those things in more!!!

If you feel insecure, it's because you haven't dealt with whatever is putting you in a negative state of mind. So, you must stop running from this problem and face it head-on.

The badges you bring into a relationship will only give you more problems to deal with in your current relationship.

The person who hurt you or made you feel less than is not the person you are currently in a relationship with.

Allow that new person to be judged on their own merit. Your new relationship will have its obstacles to overcome.

If you are feeling insecure in your current relationship and this is a new feeling, you may want to examine a few things.

This could be that your relationship isn't meeting your needs, or it could have to do with something outside your union, like a lack of self-confidence or fear of the unknown. But, again, the important thing is to get to the root of the problem and solve it together.

Seek counseling if both of you cannot figure it out together. Don't be under the impression that things will work themselves out.

Don't ignore the "Red Flag" in your mate that they don't want to do counseling!

While working on your insecurities together, you can do a few things to help the process.

Things you need to address within yourself:

- Stop saying you are insecure
- Doubt your doubts, not yourself
- Name your critic
- Stop overthinking
- Get to the root of it
- If you need help, ask for it
- Cut off your comparisons
- Cultivate confidence within yourself

The steps that you take to address your personal needs will give clarity to everything around you and the people in your life

Did you settle for your partner because you were at a low point in your life, or did they come into your life to help you face the long road ahead?

Once you remove your self-doubt, you will be able to see the actual color of the flag your partner has.

A dark or secretive past

What do you know about your partner's past? Should their past matter? Would you want to be judged on your past?

These are all questions that you must ask yourself as it relates to you and your future.

What I do know is this, it hurts to keep secrets. Secrecy is associated with lower well-being, worse health, and less satisfying relationships.

Which personality type is most secretive? It must be **INFJ**. They are highly private and sensitive and don't trust others easily.

WHAT IS AN INFJ?

INFJ stands for....

INTROVERTED — energized by quiet time alone
INTUITIVE — see patterns and possibilities
FEELING — prioritize people and emotions
JUDGING — prefer structure and order

typefinder

(INFJ) personality is someone with Introverted personality traits, Intuitive, Feeling, and Judging personality traits.

They tend to approach life with deep thoughtfulness and imagination. Their inner vision, personal values, and a quiet, principled version of humanism guide them in all things. **(This is me)**

These are not bad qualities, but they need to be understood and adapt to their current relationship so that both parties are getting what they need from the relationship.

I will use that **communication** word again that we can't seem to get away from.

There is a difference between a dark past and a secretive past. You must understand the difference between the two because if you try to combine the two, the results can be devastating to your relationship.

Non-resolution of past relationships

> *If you carry old bricks from your past relationship to your new one, you will build the same house that fell apart before.*
>
> loveandsayings.com

If you've had your heartbroken in the past, your past relationship may be affecting your new relationship. Likewise, our past can negatively affect us.

Whether that was the result of someone breaking up with us or you mutually decided to part ways.

A person who stays friends with their exes when they are in a new relationship is asking for problems and should be a significant **"Red Flag."**

One of the main reasons you're not letting go of a past relationship is that you're lonely right now or are still connected to that person's energy.

Yes, exes can be friends, but if you are in a relationship, it should be with the respect of your partner.

> **I don't want any other man but Jesus checking on my woman. (Real Talk)**

I know that many people are okay with their partner being friends with their exes, but how is this healthy for your new relationship?

Yes, they may be done entirely with their exes, but are their exes done with them? And you cannot be entirely done with your exes because you still feel the need to have a friendship with someone who failed you in at least one category.

I have a question? Do their exes have a current partner in their life? How do they feel about the relationship the two of you and you always talking and knowing about their personal business?

If they are cool with it, the partner is submissive because no alpha will allow another alpha around their partner. It is a fact that the women that I know don't trust other women like that.

Do you visit and call your old job and reminisce about the past? Instead, spend your time cultivating your new relationship and let your past be your past.

There is a reason that they are your exes. A person is more attractive when they are in a relationship with someone else. Would you please keep that in mind?

Men love challenges, and so do women. I know that I can sleep with any of my exes, so why would I want another man hanging around my lady?

If the way that you are currently doing things is working for you, please continue. But, if you are reading this book for answers, tell your exes the following:

Closing Statement

Would you please take the time to get to know yourself and your worth before deciding to bring another person into your life?

Learn to ask the tough questions to help you recognize and identify the **"Red Flags"** that are not good for you.

Move at your own pace. Learn to be okay with walking away from a person who does not have your best interest in mind.

Find out what works best for you, and don't compromise or settle for anything less than what you deserve.

The following will let you know that you have made the right decision in entering a relationship.

7 Signs of a Healthy Relationship

#1 You're Confident in Who You Are

#2 You Have Good Communication

#3 You're Respectful and Respected

#4 There's No Place for Violence

#5 You Have Realistic Expectations

#6 You Trust Each Other

#7 You Have Specific Boundaries Set Up.

A relationship will take a lot of work, patience, and time. Before you give up on the relationship, be sure to do all that you can do to make it work together.
Seek counseling!

www.ingramcontent.com/pod-product-compliance
Lightning Source LLC
Chambersburg PA
CBHW071013160426
43193CB00012B/2041